GOAT:
Women in Sports
Simone Biles
Gymnastics GOAT
HOT TOPICS
Gareth Stevens
PUBLISHING
BY KRISTEN RAJCZAK NELSON

Please visit our website, www.garethstevens.com. For a free color catalog of all our high-quality books, call toll free 1-800-542-2595 or fax 1-877-542-2596.

Library of Congress Cataloging-in-Publication Data
Names: Rajczak Nelson, Kristen, author.
Title: Simone Biles : gymnastics GOAT / Kristen Rajczak Nelson.
Other titles: Gymnastics greatest of all time
Description: Buffalo, New York : Gareth Stevens Publishing, [2025] | Series: GOAT : Women in sports | Includes bibliographical references and index.
Identifiers: LCCN 2023038194 | ISBN 9781538293805 (library binding) | ISBN 9781538293799 (paperback) | ISBN 9781538293812 (ebook)
Subjects: LCSH: Biles, Simone, 1997—Juvenile literature. | Women gymnasts–United States–Biography–Juvenile literature | Gymnasts–United States–Biography–Juvenile literature. | African American women Olympic athletes–Biography–Juvenile literature.
Classification: LCC GV460.2.B55 R35 2025 | DDC 796.44092 [B]–dc23/eng/20230925
LC record available at https://lccn.loc.gov/2023038194

First Edition

Published in 2025 by
Gareth Stevens Publishing
2544 Clinton St
Buffalo, NY 14224

Designer: Leslie Taylor
Editor: Kristen Rajczak Nelson

Photo credits: Cover (photo) Petr Toman/Shutterstock.com, (wreath) Igoron_vector_3D_render/Shutterstock.com, (banner, cover & series background) RETHELD DESIGN IRI/Shutterstock.com, (gymnastics icon) Bilal Sirrullah/Shutterstockcom; p. 5, 15, 19, 23 Salty View/Shutterstock.com; p. 7 Erich Schlegel/Alamy.com; p. 9, 21, 25 A.RICARDO/Shutterstock.com; p. 11 Dirk Waem/Alamy.com; p. 13 Danny Lawson/Alamy.com; p. 17 Featureflash Photo Agency/Shutterstock.com; p. 27 The White House/Flickr.com; p. 29 Anders Riishede/Shutterstock.com.

Printed in the United States of America

CPSIA compliance information: Batch #CSGS25: For further information contact Gareth Stevens, New York, New York at 1-800-542-2595.

Contents

Undisputed

There's no question that Simone Biles is the GOAT, or greatest of all time. Her high level of skill has led her to win, break records, and truly change the sport of gymnastics. Simone has worked hard for her success, earning many Olympic **medals** and world **championship** titles!

WHAT A STAR!

Simone is 4 feet 8 inches (1.42 m) tall. She packs power in every inch!

Family Ties

Simone was born on March 14, 1997, in Ohio. She has two sisters and a brother. When Simone was young, she and her sister Adria were **adopted** by their grandparents, Ron and Nellie. They grew up near Houston, Texas.

WHAT A STAR!

Simone has said she was brave as a child. She was always running and jumping around!

Hitting the Gym

Simone started gymnastics at age 6. She had a natural talent! By the time Simone was a teenager, she was **competing** in national meets! In 2011, Simone started competing in elite, or highest-level, competitions.

WHAT A STAR!

When Simone was 14, she left regular school and started learning at home. She trained in gymnastics for six to eight hours a day!

World Champ

In 2013, Simone won her first all-around world championship title. She was the first Black woman to do so! Simone also won the all-around title at the USA Gymnastics National Championships that year. She was just 16 years old!

WHAT A STAR!

In the 2013 world championships, Simone did a kind of flip no one had ever done before! The skill was named the "Biles." Today, there are four gymnastics moves named after Simone!

Setting Records

Simone won four gold medals at the world championships in 2014! She did it again in 2015. Simone had now won 14 world championship medals, the most of any U.S. gymnast, man or woman, ever! Her 10 gold medals set the world record in women's gymnastics too.

WHAT A STAR!

The all-around title at the world championships in 2015 was Simone's third in a row! No other female gymnast had done that since 1992.

Got the Gold

Gymnastics fans had high hopes for Simone going into the 2016 Olympics. She won gold as part of the U.S. gymnastics team! She then won the floor exercise and vault **events**. Simone got her fourth gold medal in the **individual** all-around.

2016 OLYMPICS

WHAT A STAR!

Simone also won a bronze medal at the 2016 Olympics in the balance beam event.

Simone's achievements during the 2016 Olympics made her a star across the country! She won a Kids Choice **Award** in 2016, and a Teen Choice Award and an ESPY Award in 2017. After all of this, Simone took some time off from gymnastics.

WHAT A STAR!

Simone wrote a book about her life that came out in 2016. It's called *Courage to Soar: A Body in Motion, a Life in Balance.*

Back and Even Better

Simone returned to competing in 2018. She won all five women's events at the U.S. national championships, including a fifth all-around win. Then, she won six medals, including four gold, at the world championships. Simone was now the most **decorated** female gymnast ever!

WHAT A STAR!

Simone won her first medal for the uneven bars at the national championships in 2018—and it was a gold! Before this, the uneven bars event was thought to be Simone's weakest.

The Best of the Best

In 2019, Simone won five gold medals at the world championships. With a total of 25 world championship medals—plus her Olympic medals—Simone became the most decorated gymnast ever, man or woman! Simone then set her sights on the 2020 Olympics.

WHAT A STAR!

Like all Olympians, Simone had to keep training until 2021 before competing. The 2020 Olympics were pushed back due to the COVID-19 **pandemic**.

Before heading to the Olympics in 2021, Simone did something no woman had ever done. She landed a move called a Yurchenko double pike vault. It includes two full flips in the pike position, or bent at the waist with straight legs.

WHAT A STAR!

Simone's achievement lives up to something she said in 2016: "I'm not the next Usain Bolt or Michael Phelps—I'm the first Simone Biles."

The Twisties

At the Olympics held in 2021, Simone won a silver medal in the team all-around. But during the team finals, she withdrew, or left the competition. Simone withdrew from other events too. She was having trouble with mental health as well as body awareness when twisting.

WHAT A STAR!

Simone did come back to the Olympic competition that year to win a bronze medal in the balance beam!

After the Olympics, Simone spoke out about the importance of taking care of mental health. She became a hero to many for what she said! In 2022, President Biden awarded Simone the Presidential Medal of Freedom, the highest U.S. honor outside of the armed forces.

WHAT A STAR!

In 2023, Simone married Jonathan Owens, a football player who has played for the Houston Texans and the Green Bay Packers.

Still Great

Simone said in 2023: "I've accomplished more than my wildest dreams." She's not done yet! After two years off, Simone returned to competition in August 2023. The GOAT can still go for the gold!

WHAT A STAR!

In October 2023, Simone won her sixth all-around title at the world championships!

Simone Biles Highlights

2011 Simone starts competing as an elite gymnast.

2013 She wins her first all-around world championship title.

2015 She breaks the record for most world championship medals in gymnastics.

2016 She wins four Olympic gold medals and one bronze.

2018 She becomes the most decorated female gymnast ever.

2019 She becomes the most decorated gymnast, man or woman, ever.

2021 She wins two Olympic medals, a silver and a bronze.

2023 She returns to competition.

For More Information

BOOKS

Andersen, Josh. *Simone Biles vs. Nadia Comaneci: Who Would Win?* Minneapolis, MN: Lerner Publications, 2024.

Stevenson, Robin. *Kid Olympians, Summer: True Tales of Childhood From Champions and Game Changers.* Philadelphia, PA: Quirk Books, 2024.

WEBSITES

Simone Biles
simonebiles.com
Find out all about what Simone is up to on her website.

USA Gymnastics | Athletes
members.usagym.org/pages/athletes/nationalTeamWomen.html?id=164887
Read all about Simone's history with USA Gymnastics here.

Publisher's note to educators and parents: Our editors have carefully reviewed these websites to ensure that they are suitable for students. Many websites change frequently, however, and we cannot guarantee that a site's future contents will continue to meet our high standards of quality and educational value. Be advised that students should be closely supervised whenever they access the internet.

Glossary

adopt: To make part of a family.

award: A prize given for winning something.

championship: The title of the best person or team in a certain sport.

compete: To try to win a contest with others.

decorate: To give a medal or award.

event: A happening in a sports competition.

individual: Having to do with just one member of a group.

medal: A prize given to the winners of a competition. They are often made of metal and worn on a ribbon around the neck.

pandemic: A time when a disease spreads quickly and affects many people over a large area or across the world.

Index